Our mo

by Jenny Giles
Photography by Bill Thomas

Our mom is a teacher.

She teaches preschool.

My little sister
goes to the preschool
with Mom.
I go to school.

We go to the park
with Mom.

We play on the swings.
Mom stays
where she can see us.

Mom likes books.
We go to the library with her,
and we get some books.

We go to the shops.

Mom gets some milk,
and some bread,
and some oranges.

We get
three ice cream cones, too.

We walk home.
We help Mom
with the shopping bags.

My little sister falls down,
and she cries.
Mom helps her to get up.

We all go inside,
and Mom looks after
my little sister.

We love our mom,
and she loves us.